Reflections of My Life

Widow of W. Phillip Keller, author of "A Shepherd Looks at Psalm 23"

By

Ursula E. Keller

xulon PRESS

Reflections of My Life
Widow of W. Phillip Keller, author of "A Shepherd Looks at Psalm 23"
by Ursula E. Keller

Printed in the United States of America

ISBN 978-1-60477-343-9

www.xulonpress.com

Dedication

To

My children
Gordy, Ria, Ricky and Monika
to give them a better understanding
of their Mom.

A Word of Thanks

A note of appreciation is due to my dear
helper
Eunice Myrah
who very kindly and efficiently
edited and typed my handwritten
life story.
In large measure the credit
for the beginning and completion
of this little booklet goes to my dear friend
Irma Wray.
She especially encouraged me, as well as
others, for many years to write my life story.
May it become an inspiration to my readers.

Ursula E. Keller

Introduction
and
Acknowledgment

Over the years many of my dear friends have encouraged me to write my life experiences. Now in my 77th year I will reflect on the highlights and twilights of my adventurous life.

My place of birth was a serene city in the heart of the province of Mecklenburg. Schwerin was the capital of northern Germany, called The City of Many Lakes and Forests, established some 800 years earlier. It was famous for its beautiful castle that for many years had been occupied by aristocrats. Schwerin was also well known for its state opera house and enormous museum with its more than 200,000 visitors annually. Last but not least, I remember the high towers of several cathedrals. The city was built in a harmonious blend of Gothic, Renaissance and English architecture.

Left motherless at the tender age of two, I was raised in a fine Christian orphanage. My godmother made the arrangements for my brother and me to live there. She was a lovely single lady, who was a cousin of my grandmother. "Aunt Elise" was a member of the board of the Evangelical Lutheran Church, under whose auspices the orphanage was managed.

The orphanage was on a 25-acre parcel of land. A large brick building, it was like a mansion to me. It is still well preserved with its beautifully kept grounds and a gorgeous mahogany interior. There were many fruit trees, berry bushes and vegetable beds, making it almost self-supportive.

At that time, 1931 – 1940, it was a good place to be. There we had Christian house parents and kindly "Aunties" who gave us a fair start in life. "Auntie Edith" was my favorite. She requested to have me pose for a portrait with a doll in my arms, which she kept after her retirement. But all this changed in 1940 when our staff was replaced with highly trained political members. Instead of prayers and adoration to God our Father in Heaven, we were told to worship Adolph Hitler.

1945 – the terrible World War was over. Germany's Nazism was defeated, but the Soviet Union occupied, not just Mecklenburg, but all of Germany from east of the River Elbe. Again we lived under a dictatorship, from which I escaped to West Berlin. From there I immigrated to Canada in 1951.

Like the Old Testament character, I too walked 40 years in a "wilderness." I believe now with all my heart and soul, it was by God's arrangement that I became the wife of the well-known and beloved Christian author, W. Phillip Keller.

We enjoyed a very adventurous life together for 27 years. With God's help, over 20 devotional and inspirational books were produced. They are still a blessing to many readers.

Contents

Chapter 1

Childhood Years

B orn during the Depression years gave me a poor start in life. Times were hard. An epidemic of tuberculosis spread throughout Europe. It took many lives, including my mother and my brother who was four years older than me.

Looking back on the 11 years at the orphanage makes me at times feel very grateful. I am convinced I had a better life and upbringing there than with a young father who had an alcohol problem. When I was 14, he even agreed with that, when he wrote in a letter saying, "I had no problem finding another woman, but not a *mother* for you."

At the orphanage, we children were placed in three categories – *Saeuglinge* under two years of age – the largest group, *Kueken* from two to six years, and the six to 14-year-olds in another section of this majestic building. There were always at least 50 orphans to be nourished, not just physically, but spiritually as well. Many were adopted before the age of six. There were couples wanting to adopt me too, but my father would not give his permission.

Every morning the housefather would awaken us by playing a lively tune on his trumpet. We would get dressed in our training suits for outdoor morning exercises, where we learned how to breathe properly filling our lungs with fresh air. After this, we got ready for breakfast and school.

We prayed and played together in wonderful harmony. The few boys in the orphanage were separated from the girls.

There were rules and regulations to follow, along with household duties to fulfill. If anyone went out of control, they were sent to an *educational institution*. This in itself made us obedient and very respectful of our elders.

Like most children we too were mischievous. When we were disciplined, it was without a stick. We stood in a corner with our face to the wall or we had an afternoon nap while the other children had a fun time playing ball.

One incident I recall very clearly. It came about because we wanted to be in style. All nine girls in our large bedroom wore pigtails. One evening we decided to snip off our pigtails to look more like the other girls at school. Annelie, who became my life-long friend, hesitated to do it herself. She had beautiful long hair, but was afraid of the consequences should she cut it herself. So, I did it for her. But! I cut only one of her pigtails. Obviously, the other one had to be removed too. One of the "Aunties" took her to a hairdresser to have it done professionally. We girls had a great giggle over this. Well, the next morning at the breakfast table we received an earful about being vain. I was given double punishment and was made to get on my knees to pull weeds from between the cobblestones. To set our hair in style we used paper curlers. During the air raids, when we had to dash down to the basement with curlers in our hair, the staff would make fun of us, calling us *Pfingst-oxen* [decorated cows].

At the orphanage we never experienced boredom. There was always something to do. We played ball, plus a multitude of other games. We learned to mend our own stockings, also to knit potholders and crochet scarves. They taught us to harmonize in singing folk songs and to play various musical instruments. It was all a lot of fun.

No favoritism was practiced, with the exception of our birthdays. At breakfast we received as many candles as our age, plus an extra *candle of life* on a cake we shared with those of our age group. We were raised to be modest and to share gladly with others.

The best treat of all was to be invited for dinner in the staff dining room. It just made us feel so special. To this day I still love to celebrate every birthday. It is a gift from God and a celebration of life!

Even more exciting was the Christmas season. The large mahogany folding door, which separated the living room from the dining room, was closed for a couple weeks before Christmas Eve. At that time, we were busy making gifts by hand for the staff members. Like most children, we wrote our lists of wishes for Santa, which had to be nothing over $10 [10 marks].

Celebrations started Christmas Eve. All of us over six years of age attended the evening church service. Following this, we performed our Christmas play for the staff. We recited memorized verses from the Bible and sang hymns in harmony.

While we were still gathered together, the large mahogany door was opened and for the first time we would see the lovely candle-lit Christmas tree. A table of gifts was set up. There were nametags on the presents for every child. Excitement filled the atmosphere! We felt so very blessed to receive a new dress and one of our wishes for a toy, plus an orange and a chocolate bar.

The chocolate-decorated tree remained up until New Years. Every evening before bedtime, we would walk around the tree and were allowed to take one piece of the brightly wrapped decoration. What a treat that was!

Chapter 2

Wartime

All of this harmonious lifestyle changed when World War II began. I recall, at the age of ten, reading the headlines in the newspaper:

Danzig oder Krieg!
In English – *Gdansk or War!*

Hitler's troops marched into Poland. Many people would "Heil Hitler!" Work became plentiful, though we were under a dictatorship. People were glad to recover from the Depression. The city of Schwerin was strictly residential, so we felt pretty safe. But once Hamburg and Berlin were bombarded, the sirens would scream, making us run off the streets or jump out of our beds to hurry to the shelter.

At the orphanage, strict political "Misses" replaced the good-natured Christian staff. Our "Aunties" disappeared. We were made to march, sing Hitler's propaganda tunes, and we prepared ourselves for the worst. They tried to make little soldiers out of us. Whenever Hitler addressed the nation, we were forced to listen to his radio broadcasts. We also had to attend political meetings. Only the sports events interested me.

In 1942 my father settled down, hired a housekeeper and received permission to take us home. He was anti-Nazi, more likely a Communist, so he prevented me from attending political sessions. Many times government officials threatened him, but he stood by his belief that his daughter should not be brainwashed by the Nazis. As little as I knew of my father, I know he had my best interest at heart.

Food rations were not sufficient to live a healthy life on. My 17-year-old brother suffered more than I did with the meager portions on his plate. Many a time I would hand him an extra piece of bread under the table. He always looked frail, and in 1943 he contracted tuberculosis and died six months later. The only comfort I had was to know that he died in a hospital bed and not on a field in Russia, where a lot of our young boys lost their lives. Life for me became even lonelier. And my father's housekeeper welcomed no playmates, especially those from the orphanage.

Once she was released, Annelie and I met secretly. I would visit her in a nearby town. In the meantime, I had to be content living with my father's housekeeper.

Father wasn't fit to go out to war, so the authorities made him serve as a guard for prisoners in Hamburg and Husum. With only one weekend off a month, he supervised the construction of concrete shelters. The prisoners respected him because he treated them fairly and with pity. When the war ended, father returned to Schwerin.

After my brother's funeral in 1943, the housekeeper decided to visit her parents in East Schlesien, near Breslau, which has now become Poland. I traveled along. All went well until we returned to Schwerin. Our train made a sudden stop at the small airport. Low-flying bombers smashed the terminal and machine-gunned the passengers – especially those in uniform – as they jumped off the train. We all tried to shelter ourselves behind a hedge, but many lost their lives.

During the last two years of that horrible war, more and more wounded soldiers were sent to our city. Schools were converted into military hospitals. We teenagers had to share classrooms at different schools. Before this, we were separated into girls' schools and boys' schools. But we were just glad to get some education.

Only one more time did we have a close aerial raid. It was during the daytime and I happened to be uptown near the pond. Trenches surrounded this pretty landmark, and I was ordered to jump into the trench. From there I witnessed the bombing of our rather large freight station. It was amazing how accurately the large bombs hit their targets. The rest of the city remained intact.

Finally in May of 1945 we were greatly relieved to learn the war had ended. Prisoners were released. And fortunately for us, the American army marched in with their big tanks. How we welcomed them!

However, just before they arrived, some German civilians broke into the warehouses and took all they could carry away. This left the rest of us even shorter of food. Stores closed their doors for weeks. Because money was worthless, we had to use the old-fashioned barter system to trade with the farmers. We bicycled or walked for miles to reach some generous soul who would give us food to survive. We exchanged fine linens or damask tablecloths for potatoes and milk, which were our main staples. Hunger pains rested with us for many months. But we survived!

Law and order set in after Germany was divided into four sections. The River Elbe, near Hamburg, became the boundary between West and East. Our home city, approximately 90 miles east of Hamburg, was in East Germany. The American army was recruited to go west, and we were obliged to receive the Russian army to occupy our city. No one that I knew of, made them welcome! We had heard so many horrendous stories of them raping young girls. We were not ecstatic about their arrival.

It took a while until we accepted the Russian soldiers as our *freedom* fighters. However, we did get used to them, but when some of them partied and drank too much alcohol, they really became forceful and unpredictable.

Chapter 3

My Pleasant Memories
[From 1940 to 1950]

Even though it was wartime, we still had school, holidays and other fun. Some of these vacations were spent on my grandparents' farm. Grandma, or Oma as I called her, was my father's mother. She had lost her first husband during World War I, but had remarried.

Opa [Grandpa] would pick us up by horse and carriage. I always enjoyed the five-mile ride on sandy roads through the forest to the farm.

Looking old for her age, Oma needed a cane to keep her balance. Affection was never displayed, but she treated us well. Once when I became so very lonesome for my companions at the orphanage, Oma arranged for most of the girls to come to the farm. I still don't know how she managed it. After walking the five miles, they harmonized on a few folk songs for us, and Oma treated them to home-baked cake and chocolate milk. It was such a kind gesture – I'll never forget it.

I used to occupy her guest room. When it was cool, Oma would wrap heated bricks in newspaper to warm the down quilts. Another kindness she showed was to rub my chest and back with goose fat to prevent any chest condition, especially tuberculosis. I was spared from that disease but had many other ailments like diphtheria, whooping cough, bronchitis, and an early detection of cancer.

Oma was a terrific cook. Her potato pancakes were the best! The farm bordered on a forest where I picked chanterelle mushrooms by the dozen, Grandma would fry them to perfection in butter. Yes, I have good memories of Oma, but she passed on shortly before my brother died in 1943. Though I was only a child of 14, I wore black mourning clothes for a full year out of respect for both Oma and my brother.

Sunday afternoons were always special. We enjoyed walks around the Castle gardens.

Some of the rooms inside the Castle were open to visitors. To protect the parquet floors we stepped into large straw slippers. It was great fun to glide on those slippers through the hallways like we were wearing skates.

Once in a while we took a boat trip to another island on our large lake, and were treated there with sweet drinks.

The orphanage regularly received free tickets to attend the Opera House. So, very young in life I fell in love with opera music and ballet dancing. As a young teenager, when I lived with my father's housekeeper, I earned a little money to pay for some lessons.

Though most schools were transformed into military hospitals, we still attended confirmation classes privately at the pastor's home. At Easter in 1943 I was confirmed in the Christian faith at the Evangelical Lutheran Church. In spite of war, we were able to have new clothing for this special occasion. All dressed up, 75 young people walked down the aisle to receive our first holy communion. It was a very significant day in my life. My godmother, Auntie Elise, was so proud of me and she presented me with my first bank account. She always impressed me as a real lady. Perhaps being a servant for the aristocrats at the Castle for many years, made her that way. While at the orphanage I spent some Sunday afternoons at her lovely apartment with its French provincial furnishings. She would always pray before we had tea. Only from her did I learn more about my mother, who was a seamstress by profession. More importantly, mother was a good godly person.

At the age of 15 I started my apprenticeship at the city library. This was a fine opportunity to meet other people and experience a bit of social life.

Since the Opera House never closed its doors during the war, I was able to attend ballet classes whenever time permitted. It was my dream to become a ballet dancer.

In May 1945, my second year at the library, we heard that either the Russians or the Americans were going to capture the capital city Schwerin in the province of Mecklenburg. Most of the staff at the library fled, probably into the Russian army zone. My curiosity made me stay right in the heart of town. God was good to us letting the American army come before the Russians. They were only ten miles ahead of the Russian army! Quite a number of us went out to welcome the

Americans. Chewing gum and chocolate bars were distributed from the tanks to the crowd. For the first time in my life I saw black men. Their white teeth flashed as they smiled at us, and all fear vanished. Occupying our city until the Soviet Union took over, the army lived in large white tents by one of the lakes.

The new government ordered that all books on Nazism were to be removed from the shelves and catalogues. I was put in charge of this and did my best. These books were not burned but put into the administration's archives. As a reward, I received a scholarship to attend the Librarian School in Rostock. Thus I was set free from home at the age of 18, to become an assistant librarian.

My best friend from the orphanage, Annelie, lived with her in-laws some 30 miles away. We stayed as close as sisters. To this day, we still keep in contact by mail.

When the big bands started to play again, Annelie and I would enjoy dancing. Often we had to dance together as there were seldom enough men, because most of the fellows in our age group had lost their lives in the war.

Like most women, I too remember my first kiss from a handsome man after a dance. He was a refugee from the Baltic who had survived the war but lost track of his family. He was the same age as both of my future husbands – 8½ years older than I. Later when he was reunited with his family in West Germany our relationship ended. But before he left, he came to see me dance at one of the ballet performances at the Rostock Theater, which meant a lot to me. That day was my 21st birthday. We celebrated my special day and said our final goodbye.

Chapter 4

Life on My Own

It was a wonderful feeling not to be ordered about by an insensitive housekeeper. I found a guest room on the top floor of an apartment in a nice neighborhood. Rostock was an industrial city, larger than Schwerin and it took me a while to get used to the noisy machines and traffic, and find my way to school.

My landlady there taught me the basics of cooking. We had only meager supplies which we purchased with food stamps. She and I became good friends until she passed on. Her daughter, Barbara, still keeps up correspondence with me from Berlin.

The training I received at the library and school helped me a great deal in later years, especially in Canada. Without it, I would have had to live with my father and his house-keeper until I was 21, but I had no desire to live in that environment.

During spring break, I found an ad in the paper under Employment Wanted. It was the Opera House advertising for ballet dancers. I immediately applied. But first, I went to see *The Red Slippers* performed by a Russian ballet company. Then there was the audition. I passed! I had my foot in the door!

Not fully trained or qualified as a group ballet dancer, I happily accepted one year of intensive training. I was paid for any small part I got on stage and for filling in when someone was ill. It was a hard, but exciting, life for me. To make a living, I knit pullovers, vests, etc. in my spare time at rehearsals.

Exercise classes started at 9 a.m. An hour later we had rehearsals for a variety of dances either for an operetta, or an opera and ballet performances.

In Europe, theaters were sponsored by the city or state. There were daily performances, if not opera or operetta, there would be a concert by the Symphony Orchestra. On weekends we had matinees as well. Seldom would I be free before 10 p.m. If I wasn't a part of our theater group, I would accept complimentary tickets to attend and learn from watching the graceful dancers. I enjoyed operas like Tosca and Madame Butterfly on our free evenings. To meet the soloists in person was to me a great honor.

Some evenings after 10 o'clock the Russian dancers would perform for their army. We often stayed to watch these athletic dancers.

After nine months of training I signed my first contract and remained with the Opera House for three years. I learned so much about music and dancing, as well as meeting interesting people. I call those years the happiest of my life. At that time I had little interest in church, but every night I would pray, thanking God for His blessings and to ask for His mercy.

During the summer months the theater closed for vacation. In my restlessness I sought part-time employment. Another ad in the paper took my fancy. An acrobat and juggler looked for an assistant. I went for it and found a group of eight artists touring smaller towns and villages for the summer months. This sounded exciting. I was able to dance solo besides assisting the acrobat in his balancing acts.

My partner [Hans] and I soon became friends. He taught me new tricks for his act, and all was going well. When we desired to travel past the border of East Germany, no permission was granted. Some of our colleagues had already gone to Sweden, and we also wished to follow, but the only way to get there was by boat – which was illegal.

From the Ostsee [Baltic Sea] where we lived, it was only a few hours sailing to Sweden. Hans had invested his inheritance in a sturdy motorboat; all we needed was a captain. Somehow we got acquainted with a young couple who had a small child. The fellow was a seaman. They too, were eager to leave. We agreed to sail as soon as the weather settled down.

May 13, 1950 was a sunny day. The sea was calm, everything around us looked beautiful. Not to look too suspicious we wore double clothing and carried no luggage. The men made sure there would be plenty of fuel on board.

Five of us went sailing northward. We almost made it to the international sea boundary, when we heard a roaring sound drawing closer and closer. A warning horn [loudspeaker] made us stop the engine. We recognized the Eastern Bloc police boat with their weapons on board. They searched our boat; all appeared fine until they found too much extra fuel on board. This made them suspicious of our story – "just taking an afternoon cruise." I guess it was not very convincing.

Before we knew it, we were ordered back to shore and were incarcerated. They questioned us individually and checked if we had any criminal records. Only one question remained – were we politically sound? At the end of the day, they kept the boat but let us go free. One of the officers gave me a tip – to take the next train to West Berlin as we were now in their Black Book and could end up in Siberia as slave laborers. Yes, we knew that those who were not in favor of their political system would be shipped out of the country.

It didn't take me long to decide what to do. I was then 21 years old and didn't need permission from my father. I went to see him before I left, and felt deep inside my spirit that I would never see him again. His house-keeper stayed with him until he passed away at the age of 71. For this, I want to give her credit.

Chapter 5

West Berlin – Here We Come!

Before we boarded the next train from Rostock to Berlin we changed our clothes and went separately to purchase our tickets. To prevent looking suspicious, I took only a briefcase, but it was stuffed with clothing. We tried to make it look like an overnight stay. I prayed we would not be identified.

In those days the black market was in full swing, so just a few miles before the train entered East Berlin, a group of East police officers checked passengers who looked suspicious. A few were taken off the train, but time ran out for checking everybody's passport. We breathed easier!

Since the couple with their child agreed to follow Hans and I to West Berlin, it turned out to be a great benefit. The Red Cross nurses listened to our plight and quickly directed us to a tunnel-like alley, which would lead into a West Berlin cathedral. The wall hadn't been built at that time, so we arrived in the basement where there were many others in the same predicament. That first night I slept on a table.

The next day we were advised to report to the Refugee Department. A hundred others were already in line ahead of us, hoping to be accepted as political refugees. We were told that approximately 300 East Germans escaped to West Berlin every day to apply for refugee status. It was three weeks before we were accepted, and then only with the understanding that we would find work in West Germany.

This wasn't an easy assignment. Being in the heart of East Germany, Berlin was surrounded by the Soviet authorities. The only way to get out of Berlin to the West, was to fly. We had no relatives in the West, so we waited and gladly accepted accommodations in a refugee camp. Single men and women were placed miles apart. I shared a clean room with two girls and stayed there for a few days. Then I was lucky to find a private room to rent in Friedenau. The couple with the child received a nice suite at a hotel. Hans was most unhappy to stay in the men's camp. To him it was just like being a war prisoner in Russia again.

Actually, we were very fortunate to be granted refugee status. Not that we were politically involved, but our case was taken seriously. Of course, there must have been a search for the truth in our story, such as the boat taken from us. Otherwise we would have been sent back to where we came from.

Berlin was still in ruins. They weren't looking for people in show business. There were hundreds of unemployed artists. We agreed to help with the clean up for a dollar a day. We really didn't know where to go from there.

Hans became more and more unhappy stuck in the refugee camp. I sort of enjoyed my freedom. Here I could buy bananas and chocolate bars without ration stamps.

There was only one way to free my partner from the camp, and that was to get married so he could share my abode. In those days it was just not acceptable for men and women to be roommates. We knew each other well enough, actually liked one another, so we decided to get married. We received a marriage license at the Schoeneberger city hall.

Just before the wedding day, I tracked down Auntie Hanni, the sister of my father's housekeeper. Unknown to me, she too had lost all her possessions at the end of the war, and was living in one room on the west side of Berlin. I needed her as my witness. She was a kindhearted lady and begged me not to get married so young and under those circumstances. But it was too late. I had already committed myself. Somehow Auntie Hanni gathered up a few of her in-laws and helped me make the best of our wedding day. She provided Hans with his favorite meal – liver and onions – this was considered a real delicacy. Her niece brought a beautifully decorated cake, which tasted a whole lot better than the liver and onions!

Chapter 6

Leaving My Homeland

It was 1951. Quotas were opened for refugees from the Eastern Bloc to immigrate to Canada. Our ages were right – Hans was 30 and I would be 22 shortly. We applied for a visa. Good health was the main concern. Our physician could not give me a clean record of health unless I had my tonsils removed. I submitted to this ordeal – went to a private clinic and had the long-overdue surgery.

Our departure was arranged. We flew from Berlin to Hamburg, and then traveled to Bremen to receive our visas. The Cunard liner Scythia was anchored at Liverpool, England. It took on immigrants from different European countries. We traveled through the Netherlands by train, followed by a night ferry trip to Britain. Then we all met at the International Hotel in London. Three days later we traveled by train to Liverpool, enjoying the countryside from our coaches.

Boarding the Scythia, more surprises awaited us. Being on a British liner meant most of the crew were English-speaking. Why we didn't make it our business to learn the language of the new land beforehand is still beyond me. Directions and even menus were only in English. We were fully unprepared for this. Some authorities in Berlin convinced us that in Canada, especially in Winnipeg, there were many German people. They had their own stores, newspapers, and even a German club. All would be well.

Perhaps we were naïve to think that with our occupation, there would be no problem as we would quickly get an agent to help us. How wrong we were. In Winnipeg there was only one Vaudeville Theater.

Coming back to our voyage across the Atlantic in February – after leaving Liverpool, we anchored in Ireland. Then we shipped out to the open sea. It was a rough trip. Most of us were seasick for five long days. I thought I would die! The waves appeared as black mountains hovering around us. After five days, it was smoother sailing and we felt better. The waiters in the dining room were most cooperative, making sure we ordered the right food for our upset stomachs.

On board I attended the movies where I picked up some English words and phrases. It also helped me overcome my seasickness.

After ten long days at sea, we saw the shoreline of North America. Joy and excitement were contagious! We anchored at Halifax, Nova Scotia. A large banner read "Welcome to Canada." We had made it!

Back onto a train we went, first to Montreal where some of the French immigrants ended their journey. The rest of us boarded another train traveling west to Winnipeg, Manitoba. It was a long, rather boring ride. The land lay under a thick blanket of snow. There were few trees. It looked so barren. Here and there we passed farmers' homesteads. Then we arrived at the Winnipeg railway station. I wondered what awaited us.

Chapter 7

Life in Winnipeg

And it was cold! We had arrived in the middle of winter. Cold as it was, it took me a while to wear slacks as no woman in Germany would be seen in such attire – we'd rather wear full-length coats. The snow wouldn't disappear until May.

A distant relative of Hans greeted us warmly. His first comment when he noticed we each had only a small suitcase was, "Is this all you have?" Well, I wondered what he expected of two refugees from the Eastern Bloc. We visited at his homestead north of Winnipeg for a while. It was so primitive – not even indoor plumbing! Bedrooms had no doors, just drapes. And he had been born in Canada! The well water was full of minerals

– too hard for my stomach. I had to go to Winnipeg for medical treatment. I made sure I would not return! So, my then-husband and I went hunting for work in Winnipeg. This was much harder than we expected.

We tried the Vaudeville Theatre, which let us perform as The Bartunas once a month. We practiced new tricks and managed to juggle five rings across from one another. Hans was very talented in acrobatics, balancing and juggling on his own. A lady manager approached us to perform at an auto show and at some banquets, but she only paid $25 a performance. To make a living we needed to work full time.

Because our English was almost nil, we mostly made friends with folk from Germany. Of course, we conversed in German, which was no help at all. I finally got a job in a candy factory, later on as counter clerk and a dining room waitress at fine restaurants along Portage Avenue. My husband was not so lucky. He hardly could get into carpentry work.

Our debt of $600 for our long journey had to be paid first. We were willing to do almost anything. When fall arrived, a German foreman from a bush camp talked us into working for him. I could help in the kitchen and Hans could work in the bush. He quickly learned to fall trees, remove branches and pile them up by cords. On my free afternoons I would bring him treats from the kitchen and watch him do this hard labor on his own. All was done with hand tools – no power saws were used. I found I liked the outdoors and gave up the job in the hot kitchen to work side by side with my husband. It was humble but honest work. Soon we were able to pay off our debts – made easy because there was no place to spend our wages. As soon as we thought we were ready for city life again, we returned to Winnipeg.

Early in the spring of 1952, I knew I was expecting our first child in September. I found work at a sewing factory, which paid our rent at a rooming house. It was all a most humbling experience. We had to do manual labor because of our lack of English. We tried reading newspapers and went to movies, but what we really needed was English classes.

Our first child, Gordie, was born. A tiny little fellow weighing only a little more than five pounds, but we were delighted! Our former landlady from Berlin, who was not just a hairdresser but also a Red Cross nurse, came on a six-month visa to live with us and help take care of my firstborn. Though we had only a one-bedroom suite we managed by giving her the bedroom and we slept on a hide-a-bed in the living room.

Winter arrived and no work was available for my husband. He went into a bush camp to support us. An opening at a mine came up, but I was just not willing to spend the rest of my life in a mining town, or any other place, with a man I didn't love. His response was, "Let's go back to Germany." But that was not my desire. In my heart I knew I couldn't stay with him as we both were beginning to be affected emotionally. At that point in time, neither of us knew what true love was – not how I understand it now. "It is utter selflessness as opposed to ourselves getting our own way. It is generous self-sharing as opposed to our own gratification. And it is self-sacrifice as opposed to our self-indulgence." [W.P. Keller often cited this in his Bible studies.]

After 12 years of this sort of marriage and having had two long separations, we decided to part for good. Yes, there were our children to be considered but I was young and unafraid to face the future.

I traveled west, while Hans went back to Germany where he remarried. However, he returned to Canada with his new bride a couple years later, which was good especially for the children's sake. Gordy and Monika remained in their care – making life somewhat easier for all of us. But as a mother, I longed for my children.

Chapter 8

Restless Years

It was 1962 when the children and I took the train from Winnipeg to Vancouver. I always loved living in big cities.

On the train, a retired couple took a shine to my youngest son. Ricky, as he entertained them by running up and down the aisle in the dome car. Smiling at them mischievously, he won their hearts. Soon they heard about our move to Vancouver. They insisted that I would do better starting a new life in Victoria where they resided.

I must mention here that my second child was born three years after the first one. Ria too, was a wanted child, especially because she was a girl. I had always dreamed of having a daughter to dress up like a doll, but she didn't appreciate all the fuss. Actually, she grew up much too fast. She truly was a mother's helper. If she had her way, she would have taken on her little brother, as a living doll, from day one. What a disappointment it was to her when I insisted she was too young to carry Ricky around. After all, she was then only three years of age.

By faith and goodwill we took this couple's advice and landed by ferry in Victoria. They found us a furnished suite and encouraged me to apply for a position at the public library. Fortunately, I had kept my good recommendation from the city library of Schwerin, had it translated into English, and was called for an interview with the head librarian in the Circulation Department.

The lady was a kind-hearted person. When I apologized for my poor English, she teasingly asked, "Don't you know no one talks at a library?" She hired me and I thanked the retired couple for their confidence in me. Of course, I was most grateful to be working at the library.

The following years I was very self-assured. Though I kept my belief in God my Heavenly Father, I went my own way. A small inner voice told me I was born for a special purpose. In my ignorance I tried to find it on my own. There is a saying – "We can't stop a bird flying over our heads, but we can stop it from building a nest in our hair." I think I allowed the nest building to happen and paid dearly for it.

I realized there was a void in my life, especially since I grew up without parental love. Searching for true love was very difficult because emotions can be confusing. Finding the unconditional love in another person is almost impossible. Later in life I realized this love is only found in God our Father because His love is absolutely selfless and pure. God demonstrated this kind of love by sending His only Son into the world to be crucified for our sins that we may live eternally. It takes only faith to believe this, and I do! To love God is to please Him and thank Him daily for His mercy.

Serious illness struck me when I was only 34 years of age. It was cancer – fortunately in its first stage of development, but surgery was necessary. The staff at the Christian day care center prayed for my recovery. They were kind-hearted ladies who took not just my children into their hearts and home, but I too had a place to recover. Up to this year,

I still exchange Christmas greetings with one of those ladies. She had a soft spot in her heart for my then four-year-old son. It took me three months to recover, but the library kept my job open for me, giving me half of my salary while I was off work. Amongst the library staff, I made a few friends, but there was one special person – Yvonne who was in charge of our schedules. This lady has a spirit of an angel and she and I are still good friends.

The children and I returned to our duplex a week after my discharge from hospital. My then seven-year-old daughter took over most of the household duties. I was just too weak to do it myself. When friends came for a visit, she served them tea like a young lady. It all happened during the summer months. At least she didn't have to go to school or do homework as well. To this day I am grateful to have her as a daughter. Because of my own upbringing, the boys were never domesticated. I came from a different culture. Fall arrived with its beauty in Victoria before I could return to work. My oldest son wasn't too happy with his stepmother, so he came to live with us for a while. That made four living on my salary. I worked full time with only one Saturday off each month. At first I hired babysitters, but as soon as my daughter was old enough and dependable, I was freed from that extra expense.

Sunday was family time and we made the most of it. The children were picked up for Sunday school by one of the teachers to be taught Christian living. Afternoons were spent at a park or beach. Sometimes we managed a wiener and marshmallow roast over an open fire at the gravel pit only a couple blocks from home.

It dawned on me that I should look for a husband who would be able to support us so I could stay home to give more attention and care to my children, but I didn't look in the right places.

Saturday evenings – yes, even after work, was Mom's night out! If I didn't have a date, I would join Canadian friends at a dance at the Italian Club. Dancing and music were still in my blood. It was really no place to look for a lifetime partner. And I made a dreadful mistake by getting involved with the worst kind of man. They say love is blind. To relive those unfortunate two years is much too stressful. After it was over, it took me a full year to pass through an appalling anguish of spirit.

Chapter 9

Onward To A New Beginning

It helped me a lot to be reminded of the Scripture verse in Philippians 3:13 "... but this one thing I will do, forgetting those things which are behind, and reaching forth unto those things which are before me!"

Sometimes it takes a good dose of disappointment before God receives our attention and we beg for forgiveness. He is merciful and kind, and allows those things to happen so He can change our character.

In summer it was my custom to spend some afternoons on Dallas Road down the cliff at a gravel beach. On one of those afternoons I was greeted with a friendly "Hello" from a stranger in his beach attire. With his golden brown tan he looked really healthy. He wondered if I had come to swim in the cool water. I replied, "No, I came to relax and read."

I made myself comfortable by unfolding a small blanket and a beach towel, having removed my swimsuit cover-up to sunbathe. Lying on my stomach, I got carried away reading a novel. Not having paid attention to my surroundings, I almost got caught by the incoming tide. The stranger noticed my predicament. He said, "It looks like you need some help, Little Lady." It seemed as though the Lord caused the tide to come in just at that moment so we would get acquainted.

This was really our second encounter, but I hadn't recognized him as the person I met at the library earlier. At that time I was in charge of the Book Reservation Department. He was an author and his first travel books were in great demand. He was also an avid reader and would reserve many books. Dressed like a bushman, he would come to the library to pick up these books. Being a fussy dresser myself, I was not very impressed with his style of clothing. My first thought was, "With someone dressed like him, I wouldn't even go for coffee!" How little did I know about this man and God's plan for us!

Though I didn't recognize him on the beach that afternoon, to him I looked familiar. He introduced himself and I was astonished this was the bushman with whom I wouldn't have shared a coffee break. It turned out that he was a widower and was seeking companionship.

Our first meetings were for walks along the coastal cliffs after supper. He presented himself like a real gentleman and I enjoyed our brief meetings. Actually, at first he became my tutor. He noticed my English was self-taught and he wanted to help me. I was very much in favor of his offer. His home was just a couple blocks from mine. On rainy days I felt safe enough to go to his house. Other times we met in the outdoors. He won my respect and trust right from the beginning. I was glad to have his companionship, but the way he dressed was still a big problem.

His first travel books and nature stories were printed in Britain. They didn't make much profit. He decided to follow God's will and shared his time and life experiences pastoring a small congregation. His salary was only $100 a month. My salary was a lot better, so I bought him good sport shirts [of my liking!] to make him look more like my type of man. In those days I was quite a dresser – everything had to match! Spike heels were my favorite shoes, and they just about ruined my lower back.

By and by we realized we had a lot in common, with the exception that he was born in Kenya, Africa and I came from the northern part of Germany. Though he was of Swiss-German descent, he never learned the language – and he didn't like it. My name was changed to Cheri from Ursula for the same reason. His first name was Weldon, but at the age of 19 when he immigrated to Canada, he chose to be called by his second name Phillip.

He saw in me "something striking and arresting. Despite the passing of difficult years and crushing reverses, nothing had detracted her splendid poise and erect carriage. What was true of her in a physical sense, seemed equally apparent in the realm of her spirit. There shone from her eyes and face the superb spirit of a dynamic soul vibrantly alive, still buoyant with hope." [Quoted from our first book *Hawaiian Interlude*.] I thought this very complimentary and well expressed. Yes, he had been given the gift of writing!!

Of course, we had great discussions about spiritual things. I had been baptized and confirmed in the Christian faith in the Lutheran Church in Germany. Though his forebears were Lutherans as well, he became interdenominational and was ready to serve any Christian church.

However, when we became serious in talking about the future, he wanted to give his time only to writing. To be honest, I couldn't have pictured myself as a preacher's wife. Far from it!

I gave up my favorite pastime of ballroom dancing. I went to hear him speak from the pulpit and was very impressed, as he gave messages in laymen's language. Many devotional books were written and published because of this special gift he had received from his Lord and Savior.

When the winter storms moved in, he decided to sell his modest house and purchased a Datsun truck and camper to go south. I encouraged him to go to Mexico to write a book on the desert, which he did and dedicated to me.

Chapter 10

Philip Returns from Mexico

During his vacation with a purpose, Phillip would keep me posted. Interesting letters arrived on my desk at work. He returned on my 40th birthday and we had our first public date. I was treated to a fine dinner at the Beach Hotel in Victoria.

Through his counsel I grew spiritually. We became more and more aware that there was hope for a future. So, hand in hand, we continued our evening walks.

One evening, on a full moonlight night, we sat on a large outcrop at the waterfront when he asked if he could kiss me. There are few men who would ask permission; at least I never met one before. That was the beginning of our romance.

My own children were in their teen years. I admit, even with my rather strict rules, I had lost control. In most cases one passes on in life how one was raised and it didn't work too well for me.

The oldest, Guenther, nicknamed Gordy, was picked up by his father to return to Winnipeg. My daughter, Ria, decided to live with the parents of her best friend. For little Rick it was quite traumatic to be left most of the time on his own, because I still worked full time at the library. Older boys would threaten him and make him do things that weren't right. I was advised to transfer him out of the city to a good family home. It was Phillip who helped me find a place in the country. The lady of the house came to visit several times. Ricky took a liking to her from the start. All of us visited their home and Ricky fit right in.

However, after our return from overseas missions, we learned Ricky had been treated unfairly by this couple. They had taken in another younger boy, and Ricky had to take the blame for this boys' antics. It broke my heart to see how he had suffered.

In a way I had been set free from my responsibilities when Ricky was placed in this country home, but I missed my children and shed many tears for my inability to be a full-time home-maker and mother. I kept as close as possible to them and helped them financially with all I could afford. Phillip came to comfort me, but he had plans to leave for the South Pacific when winter would set in.

In the fall of 1969, I decided to move to Vancouver to start a new life, but there wasn't a chance for me to work in my former position in the library. Perhaps I had earned my dreamed-of vacation to Hawaii.

New Years 1970, Phillip and I became officially engaged. Phillip had just turned 49. I was eight and a half years younger, but that didn't bother me as I had little interest in younger men. Perhaps I looked for a fatherly figure. It surprised me one day when I compared a photo of my father with Phillip. They looked so much alike, they could have been brothers!

Phillip was eager for his children to meet me. We took a train to Edmonton. I stayed with his married daughter and he visited with his son. His children treated us with kindness and goodwill. But – it was bitterly cold! The thermometer kept dropping, until it stood at

32 degrees below zero when we departed a couple days later.

Chapter 11

My First Glimpse of Hawaii

Phillip shipped his truck and camper to Honolulu, and both of us boarded a plane. It was a nasty day in Vancouver when we departed. As we climbed through the gray clouds to clear sunshine above, we knew it was a wondrous omen for a new life ahead.

While waiting for Phillip's truck and camper, we rented rooms at a reasonable hotel a block from the beach. It was heavenly to walk every morning on a sandy beach and have a daily swim in the ocean.

Not wanting to waste any of my vacation time, I checked out the employment situation to see if there would be a job like a live-in housemaid. I found a suitable position with a doctor and his wife to care for their two-year-old daughter. They offered me their guest quarters and sufficient salary, so I could live comfortably in Hawaii outside of Waikiki.

However, I needed to make sure my children were happily settled. So, I returned to Vancouver, where I rented a small furnished suite near Stanley Park. After visiting with my children, and finding them content, I went back to Hawaii. In the late '60s and early '70s one could purchase a midweek return ticket from Vancouver to Hawaii for only $135!

Phillip awaited my return, but neither of us had peace of mind to make Hawaii our final stop at that time. Camping all year round was really not my thing as I was a typical city slicker. I returned once more to Canada to see the children.

Although we had broken our engagement, Phillip and I remained more than good friends and kept in close touch. We had deep feelings for one another and I knew we were in love. But one cannot live by feelings. We had to consider the fact that we came from two different worlds. Phillip's lifestyle did not impress me and he had problems with my past. But, where there is a will, there is a way – so they say.

The last note I received from Phillip, back in Vancouver, was to tell me he had decided to go home to Africa. Arrangements were made for his transportation by ship. My reply was simply that I wished him well, but I had decided to take the job at the doctor's home on July 15th.

With peace of mind, I took the jet once more to Hawaii. Arriving July 2nd of 1970, I thought I'd enjoy myself like spending time at the International Market, etc., until the middle of the month. What I didn't know was that during a Canadian mail strike Phillip's last letter hadn't reached me before I left.

He stated in that letter, as I later discovered, he just couldn't go on without me and had sought advice. Pastor Hammer, the pastor of one of Waikiki's well-known churches, explained to Phillip that only by the grace of God are we forgiven and accepted. Therefore, in the sight of God, my past was forgiven. [Some Christians are still very small-minded on this.] The pastor encouraged him to invite me back to Hawaii and marry me. Then he would have a consultation with both of us.

His truck and camper had been loaded on the ship, but Phillip cancelled his trip to

Africa, which must have cost him a pretty sum.

With his strong belief in miracles, Phillip assumed I received his last letter with a written proposal. Unbelievable as it may sound, we met in a pedestrian crossing at the International Market. My first question was, "What are you doing here? You wrote that you were off to Africa."

Before I knew it, he walked me to the pastor's office to confirm his intentions. The pastor took a good look at me and said, "Phillip, what is the matter with YOU? This girl has a spirit of an angel." Wow! In later years, Phillip would quote Pastor Hammer's impression of me when my attitude wasn't quite angelic.

Phillip must have lost ten pounds during my absence. My heart reached out to him and I was convinced that God our Father had arranged everything. It was not easy to cancel out on my employment, so we did it by mail, and I still wonder what they must have thought of me.

July 7, 1970 was the beginning of our life together – for better or for worse. Phillip being a romantic fellow, made sure our wedding would be at 7 p.m. [Somewhere in the Bible seven is indicative of perfection or completion.] Oh yes, he had gathered witnesses from the beach, but we had no family members present. I have always been grateful that we gave our vows at the altar in the Prince of Peace Church. It all went too quickly, but I believe it was God's will for us to spend the next 27 years together – until Phillip was called to his Eternal Home.

Suddenly I found I enjoyed camping with him, but figured it may be over once his book on Hawaii was completed. Overnight I also became his typist. Hawaii was all I had dreamed of. Its natural beauty and delightful climate was most intriguing to me. Yes, I could have lived there all year round, but real estate values made it prohibitive. We remained camping.

Our good pastor in Waikiki needed volunteers to help establish a camp for young people on the big island of Hawaii. We accepted this challenge and spent several months on the northern tip of the island. It was very humid and when it rained, it poured. We had a chance to get to know the local people and enjoyed the stillness and privacy on this chunk of land.

However, Phillip had problems dealing with the humidity which could have made him very ill due to having had malaria many years earlier.

What next? City life was not Phillip's cup of tea. As soon as the builders took over, we were gone.

Chapter 12

Our Journey Down the South Pacific

Phillip had planned to explore more territory, visiting other islands to gather material for his next book. I was a bit apprehensive, but now as his wife, I followed his desires and was reminded of Ruth's words in the Old Testament. "Where you go, I will go, and where you stay, I will stay. Your people will be my people and your God my God...."

Our morning devotional times together taught me a lot. My former belief was, quite simply, as long as my good deeds outweighed the bad, I'd be accepted into heaven. However, I soon found that doing God's will is far more important than having my own way. And

God's will is for us to accept Jesus as our personal Savior.

Fiji was our next stop. It was even more humid there than on the northern shores of the big island in Hawaii. A young couple, former acquaintances of Phillip, were very kind. They gave us a quick tour around the island. The turquoise sea was gorgeous. White sandy beaches invited us. All this beauty – but the climate wouldn't agree with me. The pesky mosquitoes plagued us so we had to sleep under a net.

Arrangements were made to go on to New Zealand where Phillip wanted to visit another missionary couple. The truck and camper took longer than expected to clear customs, so we attended church services of a different nature with these dear friends.

Phillip was eager to see the rest of this beautiful country. The truck and camper survived the long journey, and again, we used it as our home. It had no plumbing facilities so the sea was our bathtub most of the time and the bush became our lavatory. Sometimes there were public facilities where I could wash my hair. Salt water isn't the best for shampooing. I overcame my pride and learned to be contented without the usual comforts.

Handwritten manuscripts from Phillip kept me busy at my portable manual typewriter. At first it was very hard to read his writing, especially when it came to e, i, o and a. By the time several of his books were published, I could easily read his handwriting, and it was a joy to work together.

New Zealanders had never seen a camping outfit like ours and would follow us to get a better look. They traveled with their old-fashioned caravans. Because of our British Columbia license plates, we were invited into a few homes. They liked Canadians – even with a European accent.

The cost of living was very economical. We could live comfortably on a tight budget of $150 a month.

Phillip adored the green hills and the thousands of sheep on the lush rolling land. It brought back memories of his shepherd days. Actually, his experience with sheep behavior made him first preach, but later on write a book about it. That book, *A Shepherd Looks at Psalm 23*, became a bestseller. It had been written in the camper at the lookout in Beacon Hill Park in Victoria after his return from Mexico. In 1972 the book was released and really helped our standard of living.

We wondered if God wanted us to stay in New Zealand. Property values were favorable. All we had to get used to was – north was south, and south was north, and talking like the natives about a "fortnight" instead of our familiar "two weeks." Also, being invited for tea was supper, not an afternoon refreshment time.

Chapter 13

God's Call to Australia

After five months in New Zealand, a message arrived from a young man whom Phillip had met at a summer camp in Canada years earlier, begging us to come to Australia and help establish a camp for university students. Richard had been an Anglican rector, but longed to get out of pastoral ministry to oversee this new assignment.

The camper was shipped, and we flew to Australia. It was a much longer stretch from New Zealand than we had anticipated. We received a warm welcome. But then I became homesick – not just for my children but for Canada.

In his book on Australia, Phillip wrote two chapters on our experiences there. Not to be repetitious, I won't go into it any further, except to say the good Lord delivered us from there in time.

Phillip almost lost his life with a heart attack, and nearly lost his sight from the poison pollen of a eucalyptus tree in the yard.

Living 32 miles south of Canberra, life was not easy. One pleasure I had was playing piano in the main house. My audience was the cows, attracted from the fields by the music I played. Another joy was the many birds – beautiful rainbow-lorikeets flying about and white cockatoos resting on our fence posts at the 600-Mile Ranch.

Finally, the young men and their families from Sidney took up residence at the ranch, and we were free to move on.

An unexpected letter from the pastor in Waikiki, invited us to meet him in Sidney. He was leading a tour across the South Pacific. We were eager to leave!

Pastor Hammer's visit to the New Hebrides was most profitable. He was given 1,000 acres of raw jungle to establish a training center. Phillip was asked to study the site because he was also experienced in land management. After that, Pastor Hammer invited us to come back to his church to conduct Bible classes.

I was delighted! New Hebrides was quite a unique experience. Natives still lived in grass shacks. To swim in water 85 degrees above sea temperature was like taking a warm bath. This I would call a tropical climate.

Before we left Australia, we disposed of the camper and truck. Finally, we started living in a more civilized way. Gypsy days were over.

"Aloha" to Hawaii! It had become my third home – my favorite place on earth. We couldn't stay long as we had to ensure our Canadian citizenship by returning to Canada. I was happy about having to return. My prayers were answered!

Chapter 14

Our Return to Canada

After two long years I was able to reunite with my children. The oldest, Gordy, came from Winnipeg to see us in Victoria where we house sat for a former parishner of Phillip's little church.

The search for a permanent home went on for nearly three months. Vancouver Island was out of the question, so inland we went to find a more reasonable house in the Okanagan.

For transportation, Phillip purchased a rather old camping outfit. Winter set in and it became quite uncomfortable to live on the road.

On Sundays it was our custom to listen to a church service on our little battery-operated radio. The young minister from the Penticton

First Baptist Church had quite a good message, so as soon as we would be settled we decided to attend his church.

The Lord led us to settle in Penticton. To our amazement there was an ad in the real estate section of the local paper for a house which suited our budget. In short order we were able to move into a four-bedroom house with a massive stone fireplace in the living room. My thought was – there is enough room for at least two of my children. That wasn't meant to be. Ria planned to get married and Ricky chose to live with his sister rather than with us. We accepted their decisions and kept in close touch.

Our first furnishings were the camper cushions. Fortunately, the former owner left his kitchen table and chairs, and a dear couple offered us a full-size bed. But we really had to start from scratch.

We made our way to the First Baptist Church the first Sunday. People welcomed us very warmly. Quickly we made lifetime friends amongst them.

When *A Shepherd Looks at Psalm 23* became popular, Phillip was chosen to be the leader in many home Bible classes. God our Father blessed his ministry.

Phillip's desire to be a landowner fulfilled itself in the spring of 1973. Soon the house was sold and he purchased 16 acres with only a fruit-picker's shack on it. Seeing him so happy, I rejoiced as well, helped clean up the place and made it our home.

Then the church appointed him to take the early morning service. So, back to the pulpit he went. To do God's will, the 16 acres had to be sold and we rented a condo in Penticton.

Later on we actually were able to purchase lovely homes, one was large enough to have home Bible study groups of 75 in our rumpus room. My husband was very wise in real estate business, making several good deals.

Phillip rewarded me for typing his manuscripts by giving me a holiday at Disneyland, California. What fun I had with my travel companion Shirley, who lived at that time in Kaleden, B.C. about nine miles south of Penticton.

Another trip granted me was to return to my birthplace in Germany. Forty-one years had passed since I felt free to visit Schwerin, in East Germany. When the "Curtain" opened, East and West Germany became one country.

The time to visit was right and safe. It was 1991 when I boarded the KLO to be on my way.

I was especially happy to be reunited with my great friend Annelie. Over the years we had kept in close contact by mail.

We tried to relive our childhood years. Annelie and I knocked on the door of the orphanage and were surprised how few changes had been made. It was now a day care center for children, but the interior was still the same. I also had the pleasure of meeting her extended family. They were very kind to me, in spite of my poor German language. After three days I was amazed how my mother tongue responded. Having extra days, I explored the southern part of Germany. The town of Lindau on Constance Lake, impressed me most.

Phillip didn't mind when I asked for a brief holiday in Hawaii with my daughter Ria, who was then semi-invalided. Whenever a grandchild was born, I also went to be with my children for the happy occasion.

It appeared that a full-time ministry at the local church had to be given up as Phillip's writing would reach a much larger audience than teaching Bible classes. So we started taking three months leave of absence every winter for writing and typing.

Publishers became aware of Phillip's gift for writing devotional and inspirational books. Before he knew it, his books were on the bestseller lists. It amazed us how life changed when he became popular.

Chapter 15

Winters in California

First with truck and camper, we made those 1,300 miles to Santa Barbara in two and a half days. Later we could afford to stay at a reasonable motel. Phillip just loved the sandy east beach. He would go there to meditate when writing a book.

We were invited to booksellers' conventions. Phillip was only willing to go when he could address the enormous gatherings, sometimes as many as 3,000 people. Many nationalities, booksellers and authors would be present.

It was interesting for Phillip to receive requests from various churches to address their congregations.

Those were wonderful years. Soon it became Phillip's full-time job to travel and to write. On the road – again! But things had changed. No more campers. We were treated with accommodations in fancy hotels or beautiful homes.

These travels were unique, especially for me, as I had the privilege of meeting presidents, vice presidents and editors from different publishers, even authors and movie stars like the Rogers. Meeting Dale Evans in Waco, Texas was a delight, as at 70, she still sang her favorite tunes. Joni Erickson shared our table at one of our fancy dinner parties in Denver. It was a great honor to be invited to her movie premier.

There was one very special event in New York. Phillip had been invited to be guest speaker at a church in Newark. Before we went on this long journey, the pastor phoned Phillip to ask if there was something the congregation could do for his wife. He told him I was very fond of opera and if it would be possible, a matinee at the Met would be a real treat.

A life-long dream came true when I went with the church secretary to the Met for an evening performance of Madame Butterfly – my favorite opera.

God blessed us with many life-long friends.

In Santa Barbara, California we were practically adopted by Lynette and Jay Jordano. They treated us like family, and even now when I'm a widow they are loyal friends.

Lynette and Jay would always include us at their Thanksgiving and Christmas dinners. When they were posted elsewhere, like Colorado and Maryland, they would meet us wherever Phillip was engaged. They have been blessed to have their three boys married to fine Christian girls, and they now enjoy their grandchildren. I will always remember our good times together playing games and going on picnics. Yes, they enriched our lives – especially while we were in California without our own family.

The Lord surely had His hand of mercy on Phillip's and my life together.

Chapter 16

Phillip

No one would have expected that Phillip was an unwell man. With a year-round golden tan, he always looked so healthy. I have called him a real sun worshipper. When he would lay outside to have his sunbath there always were notes for a new message or manuscript beside him. Even then he didn't waste time.

The only vacation Phillip allowed himself was in the year of our 25th anniversary. I made sure he would choose where we should travel. Alaska had been his dream for a long time. He found reasonable cruise rates, made reservations and we left Vancouver, B.C. for Glacier Bay. The weather was perfect. When we arrived in the Bay, the captain gave the

Sunday morning service, and said, "Very seldom is it a sunny day at the Bay, we are very blessed."

We reveled in being spoiled on this cruise ship. I am very grateful that God our Father allowed us this pleasure. All other trips were engagements at conventions and churches. Phillip was not really too fond of meeting new people and speaking in public. By and by he overcame his shyness and started to enjoy meeting people of all nationalities.

He was truly a humble man. When he addressed congregations at various churches, he took his appointments very seriously. Only a few saw the happy, fun-loving side of his personality. Of course, I was one of them.

Phillip had special eating habits. He would never do without his coleslaw. Vitamin pills were taken by the dozen. He also made sure my hand wasn't too often in the cookie jar, because he wanted me to stay slim and healthy. At times he would chase me around the house when I would sneak a treat. We'd both collapse laughing. When weather permitted, hand in hand we would take a walk after supper. He was somewhat controlling and eccentric, but his good nature outweighed everything.

As mentioned earlier, I loved to dance, especially to classical music. Phillip had never been exposed to any sort of dancing, not even ballroom. He did love ballet. We had gone to see the Nutcracker and Sleeping Beauty. Sometimes he turned on a Johann Strauss tape and begged me to dance for him. I kept this up until I turned 65. By then I was suffering with high blood pressure and tendonitis and I felt inadequate dancing the ballet steps. I just wasn't graceful enough anymore. Unbelievable as it seems, Phillip copied my dancing. Even though it was funny, he was truly good at mimicking me. He sure had the straight legs for ballet!

Yes, we had a lot of fun together. Our friends were delighted when I'd suggest we play a game of Pit after I had served them a meal. While playing, our true personalities would come out. Phillip would bring us to hysterical laughter, especially at the Jordano's home.

This all came to an end after Phillip completed his 50th manuscript. At the end of June, he suddenly had a strong desire to visit Santa Barbara. This time, he drove alone from Canada, down the west coast on Highway #1. I went by plane, as each trip I found it harder to sit in the co-pilot's seat sometimes for four hours before he would take a break.

Waiting for him in Santa Barbara, I got busy cleaning up the place we were going to occupy.

Phillip was happy to arrive, but looked rather worn out. The trip had not been a pleasure. Most of the time there were fog clouds, and the road was not in good shape and was dangerously winding.

As usual, he would take his morning walk on the Goleta Beach. One day he came home soaking wet. He explained that the tide had come in and he had almost not enough strength to get through the waters. I ran a hot bath and gave him a good rubdown.

Phillip's healthy appetite diminished. He was sure he had picked up a bug. A few days later he started to look really exhausted. I encouraged him to see a doctor or to call his former missionary doctor friend in Summerland, B.C. The doctor's response was, "Phillip, you have only two choices – either come home or go to the emergency in Santa Barbara." Phillip made the right choice and returned to Canada.

Lynette, who then lived in Boston with her husband, made flight arrangements for us to fly home the next day. By then, Phillip's strength declined because he hadn't eaten properly for a week. We had to put him in a wheelchair to board the plane.

Hours later we arrived home, warmly received by a couple from the congregation where Phillip gave his last Bible classes. He ended up in emergency in the Penticton hospital, where he received intravenous and had X-rays, which proved that a massive growth had obstructed the colon. Major surgery would be necessary at once.

Phillip had never spent a day in hospital as God had performed real miracles for him. But this serious condition would give him only a day or two to live.

The intravenous did wonders. Phillip gained enough strength to remove himself from the emergency room and demanded to be discharged. I had promised him years earlier that if ever he would need care I would do it at home, not in a hospital.

Anyway, to make a brief story even shorter, he signed himself out of hospital. I was sure he would live with this cancer tumor for at least another few months.

However, the good Lord, Phillip's Savior, took him Home to Himself only four days after the diagnosis.

Phillip left a legacy not many have accomplished. In his years of writing, he contributed most of his book royalties to seven different Christian organizations. I still receive notes of appreciation from many readers of his books.

Some of my Penticton friends – Marie, Isobel, Shirley and Pegi – are all true friends who reached out to me when times became tough, especially after Phillip's passing. Isobel, who also has experienced widowhood, was at once by my side and even helped me move to Kelowna. After I was settled we had wonderful outings together, even celebrating our 70th birthdays at West Edmonton Mall. Up to this time, she still comes from Penticton to visit.

May God, through my condensed life story, bless you readers, give you hope and contentment in the crises of life.

I thank Him for all the benefits bestowed on me, and I know He has been with me always – and won't ever fail me.

Praise His Name!!